Black Santa Coloring Book

Tara Kamiya

illustrated by Liudmila Koshechkina

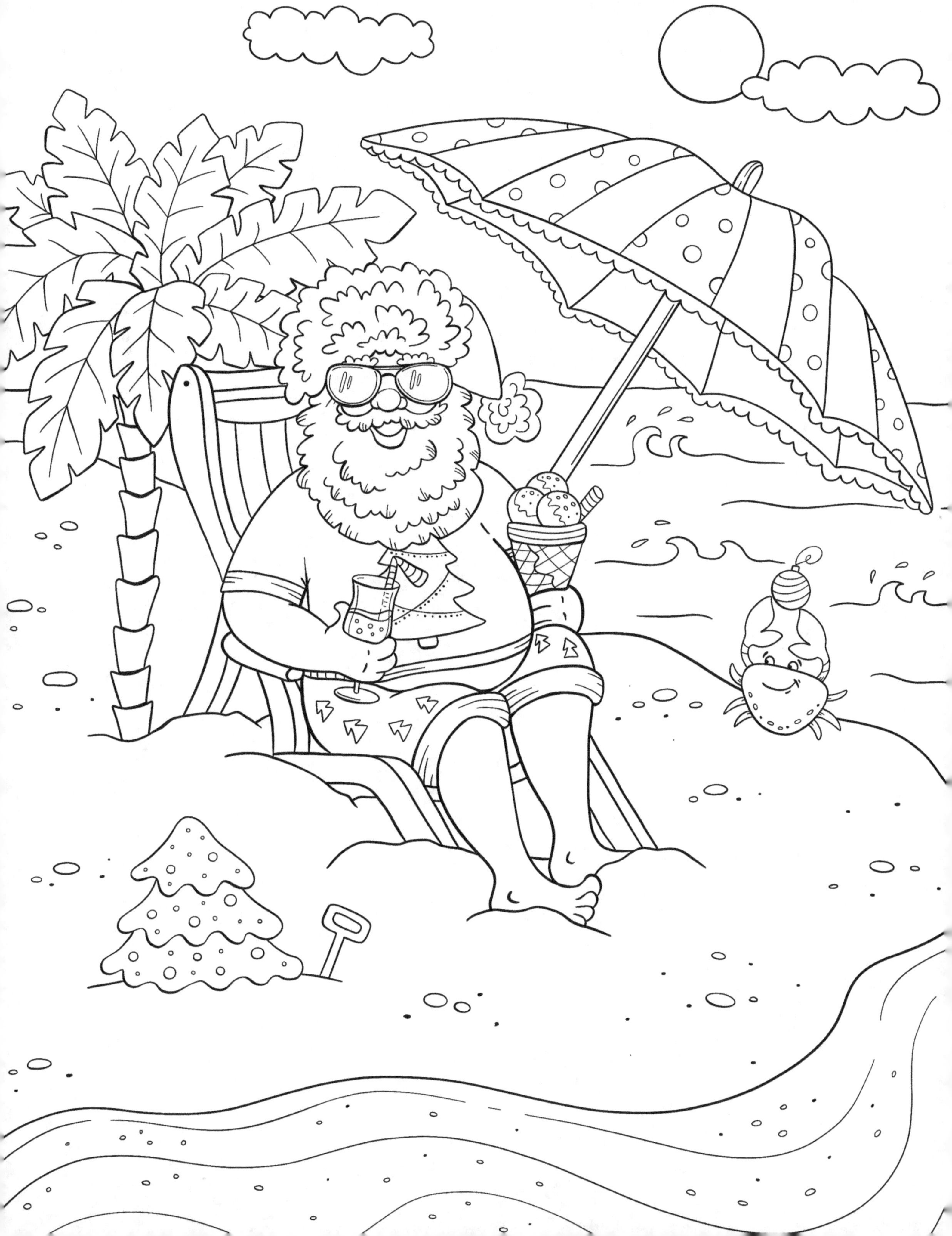

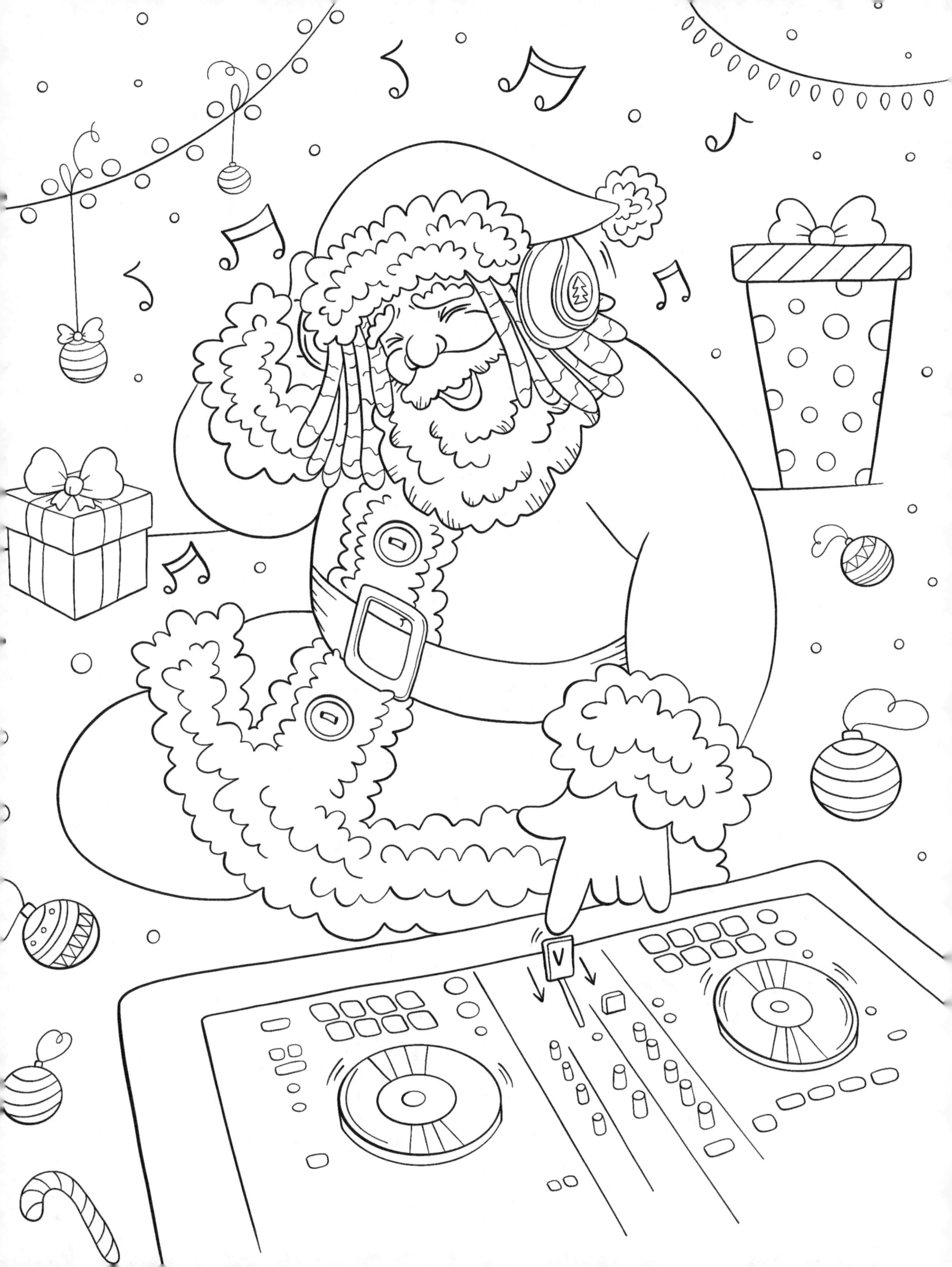
V

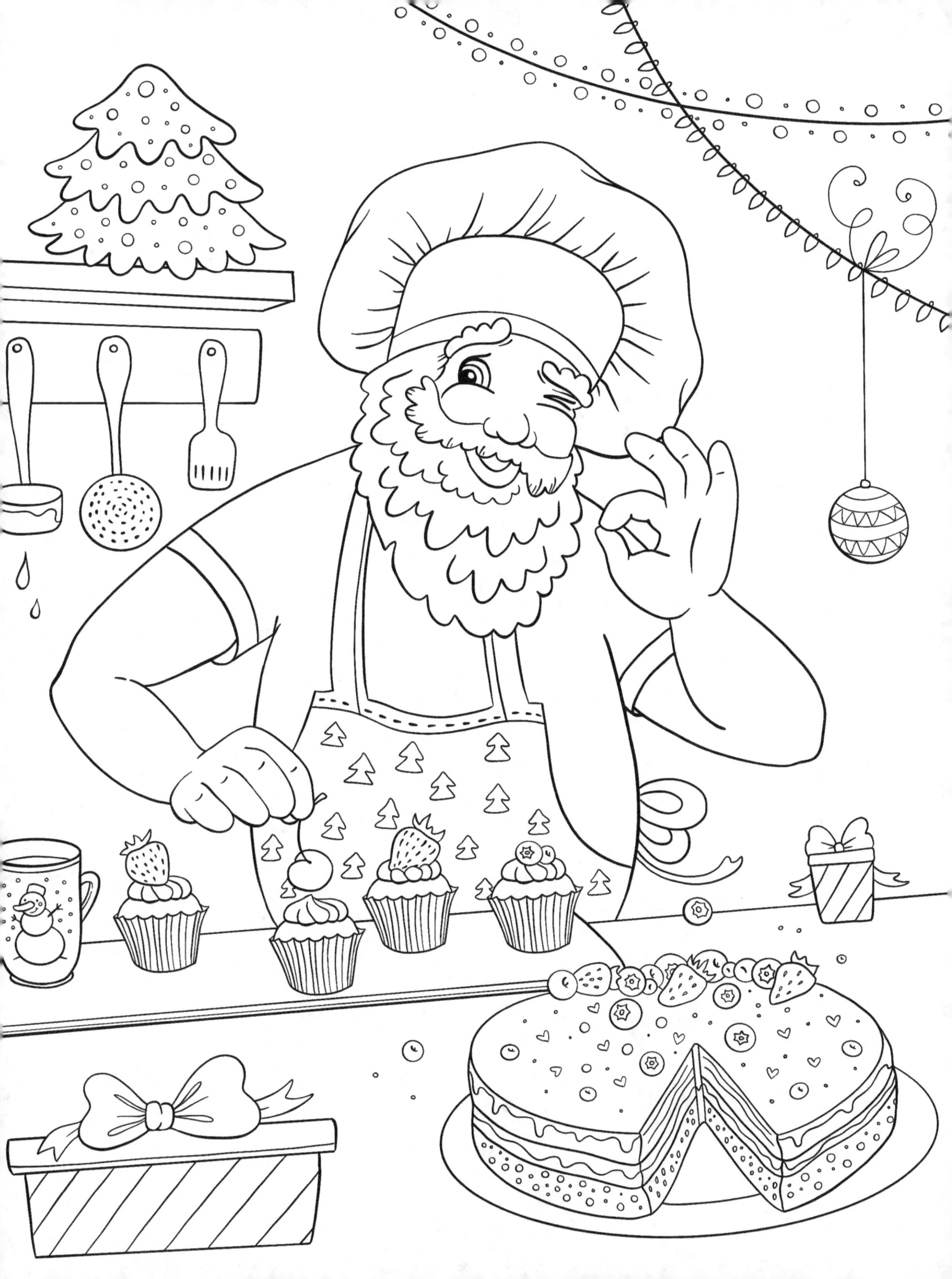

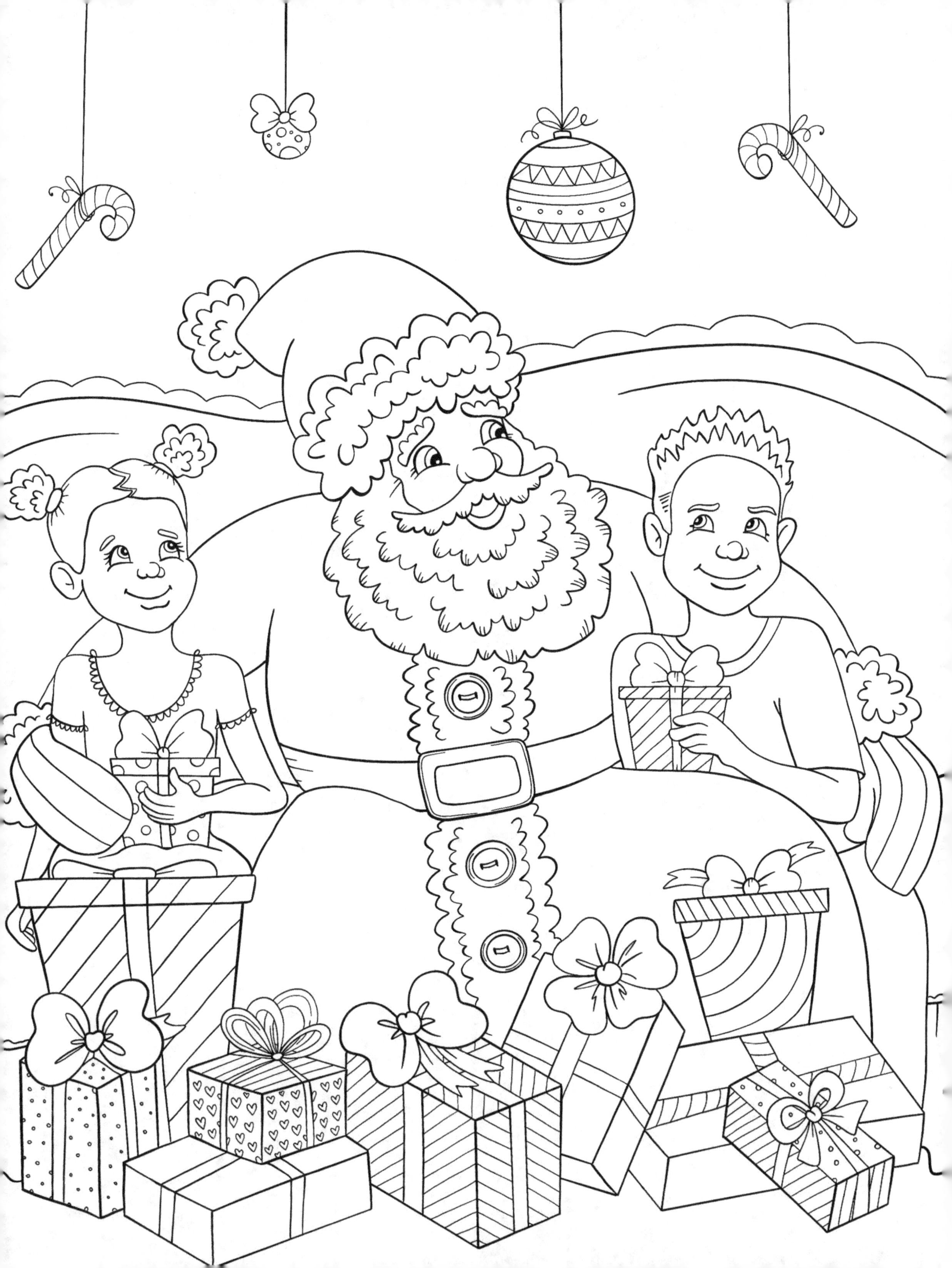

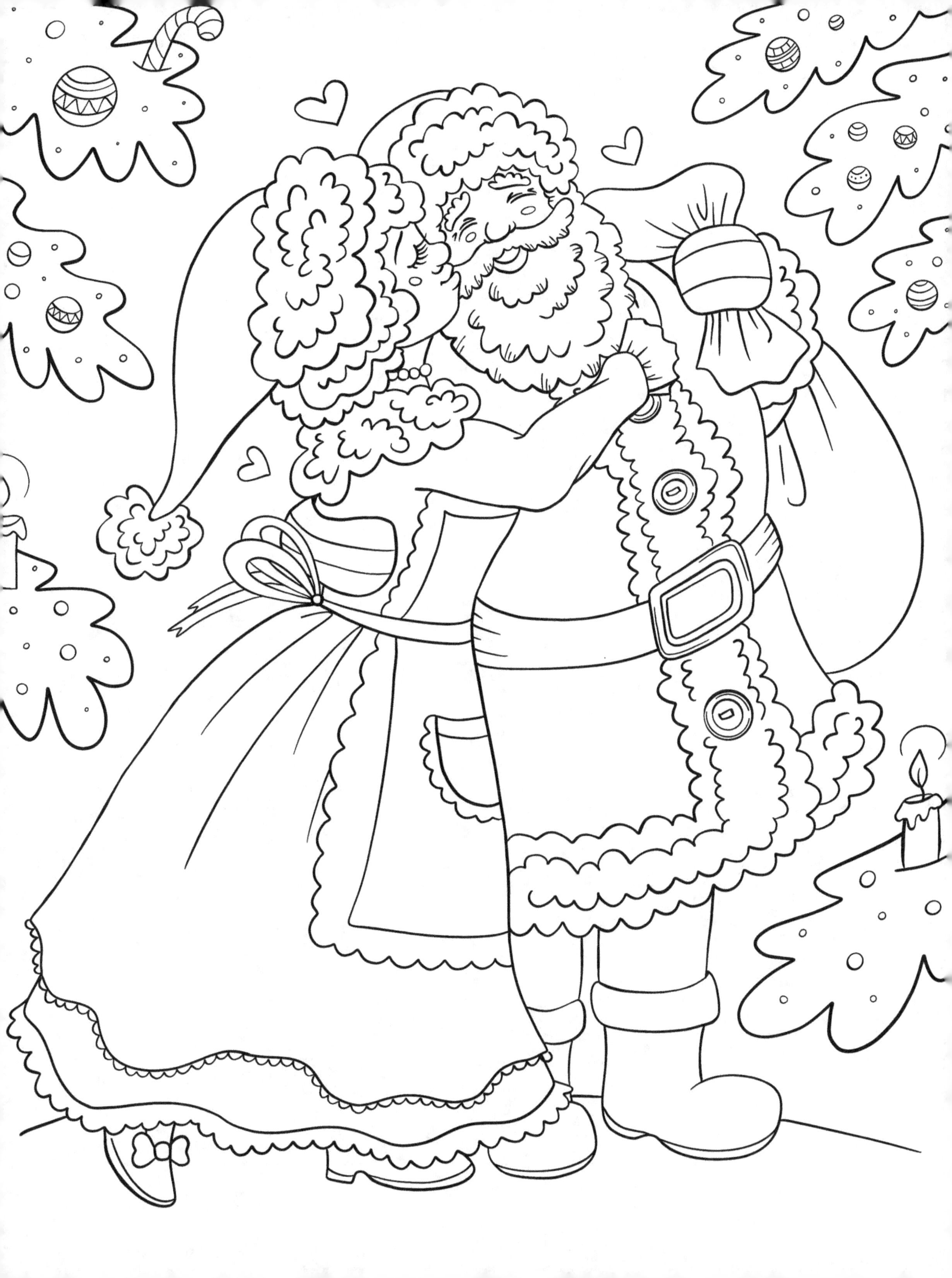

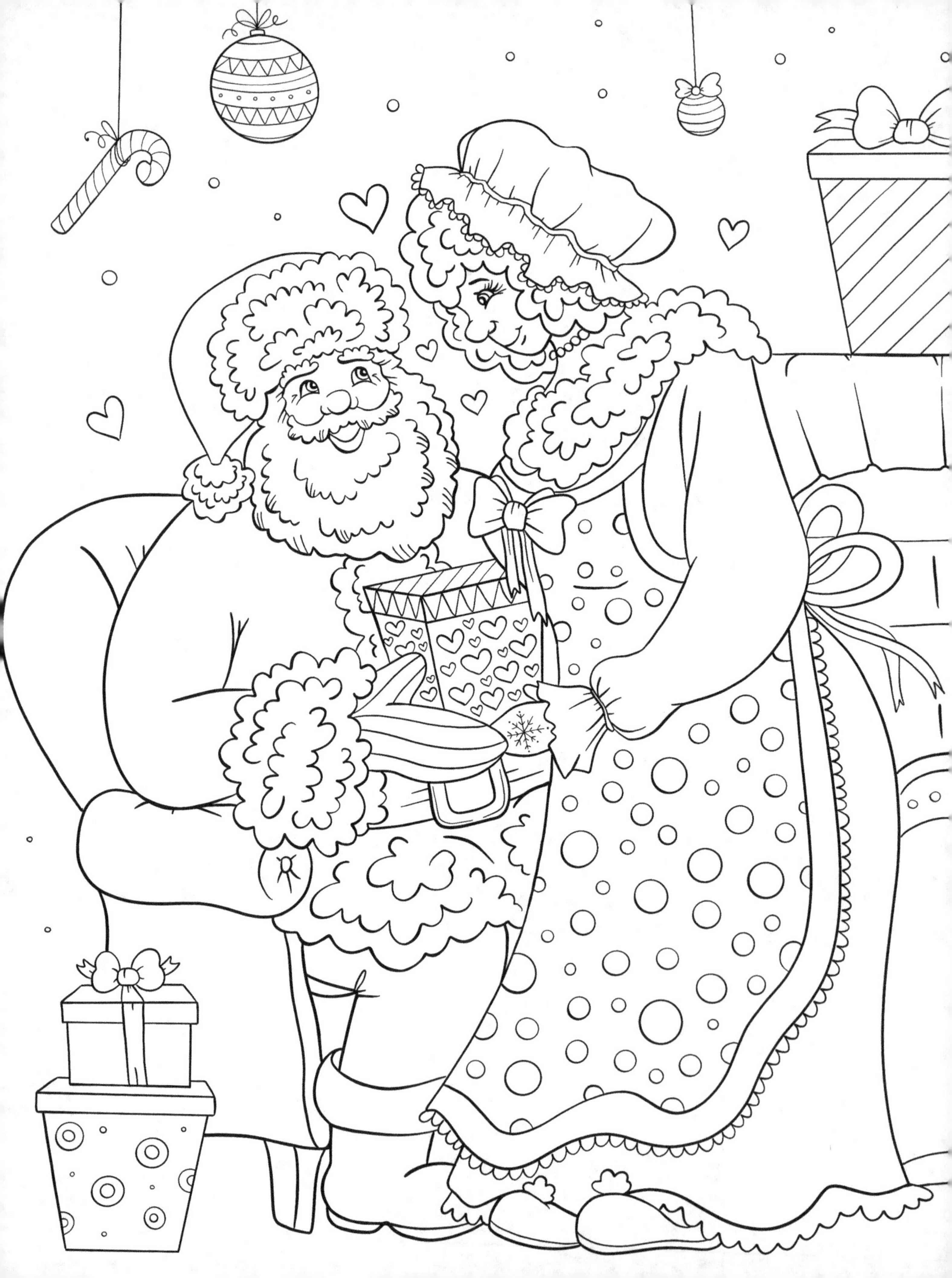

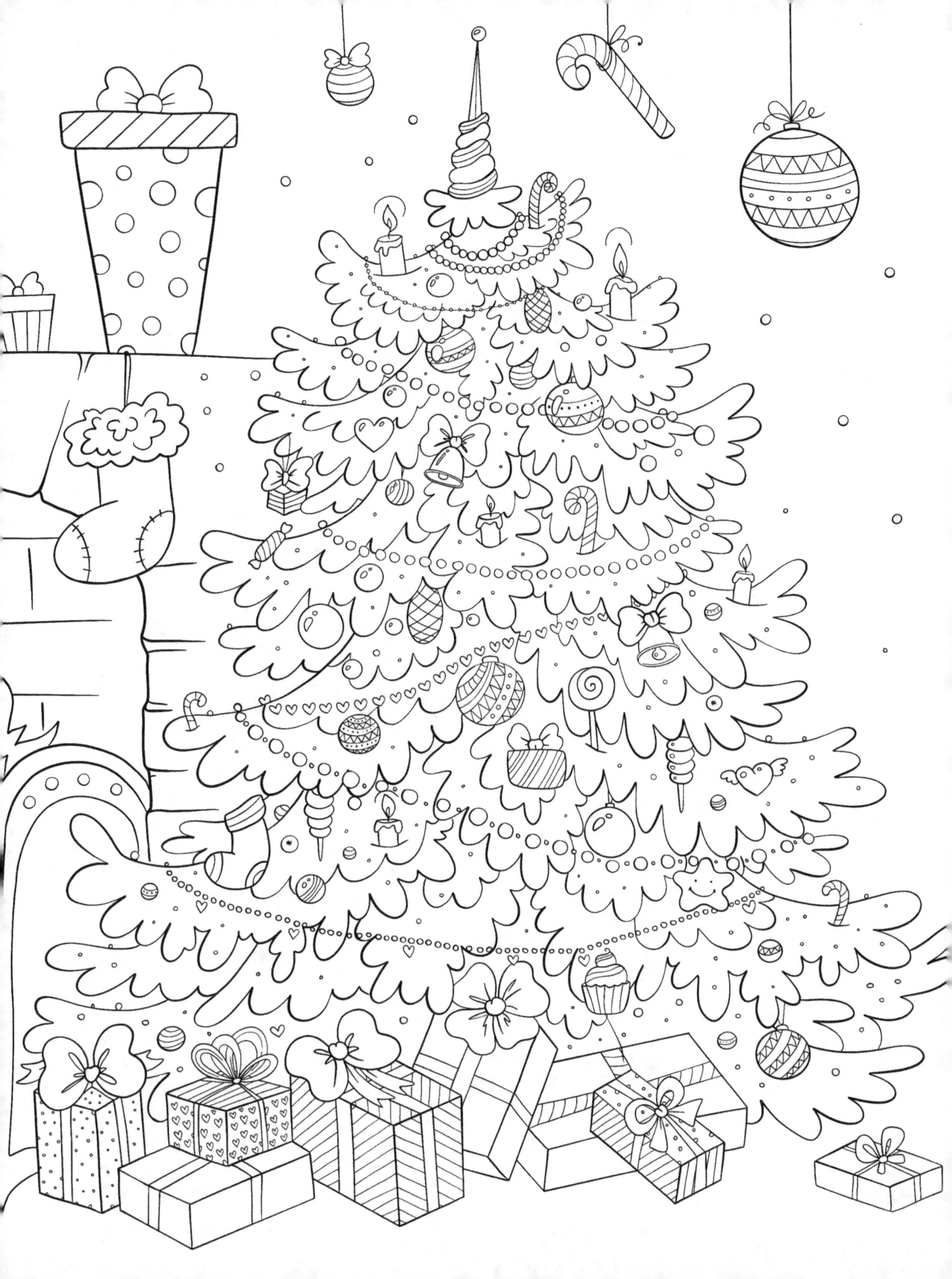

for you

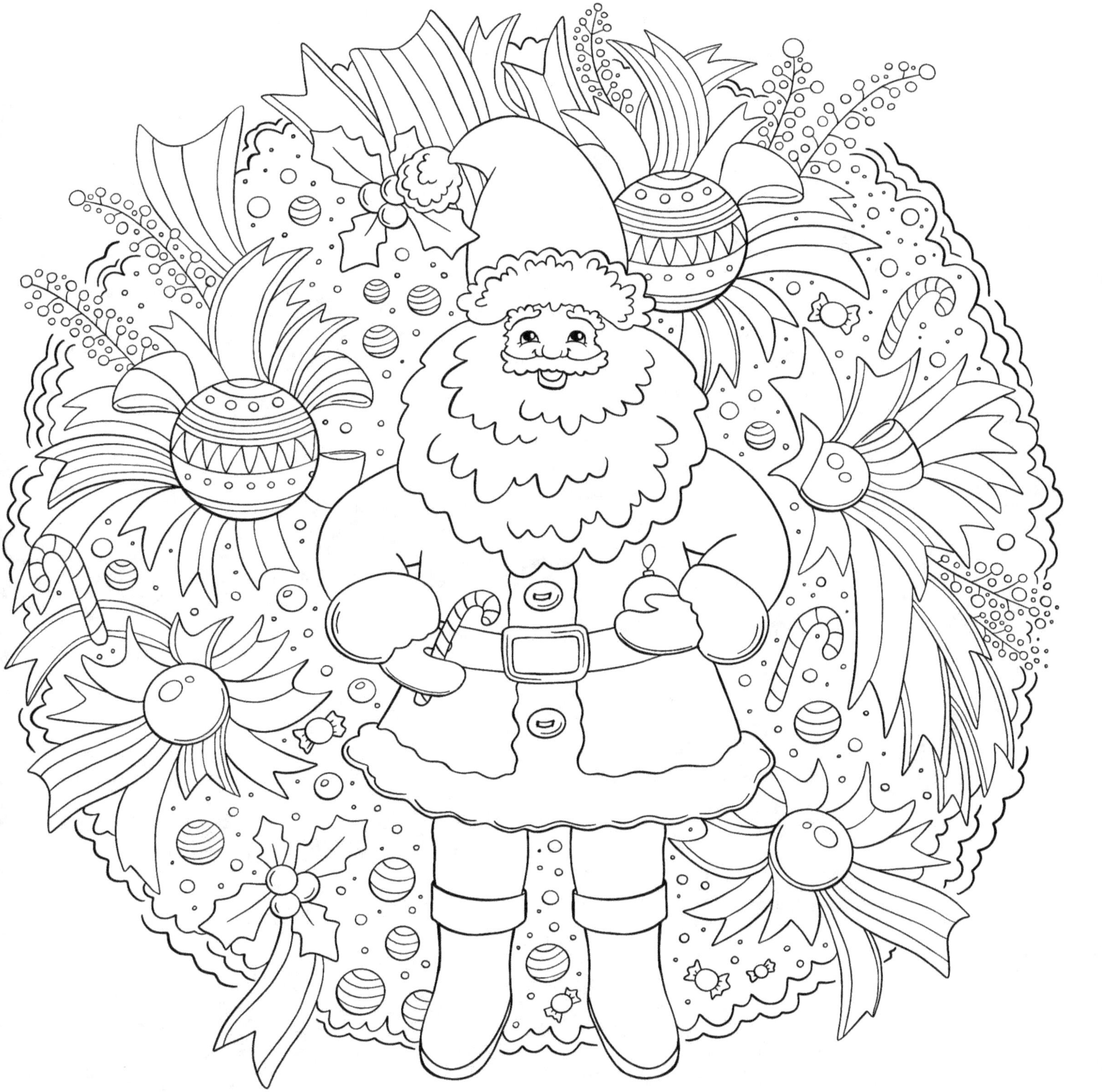

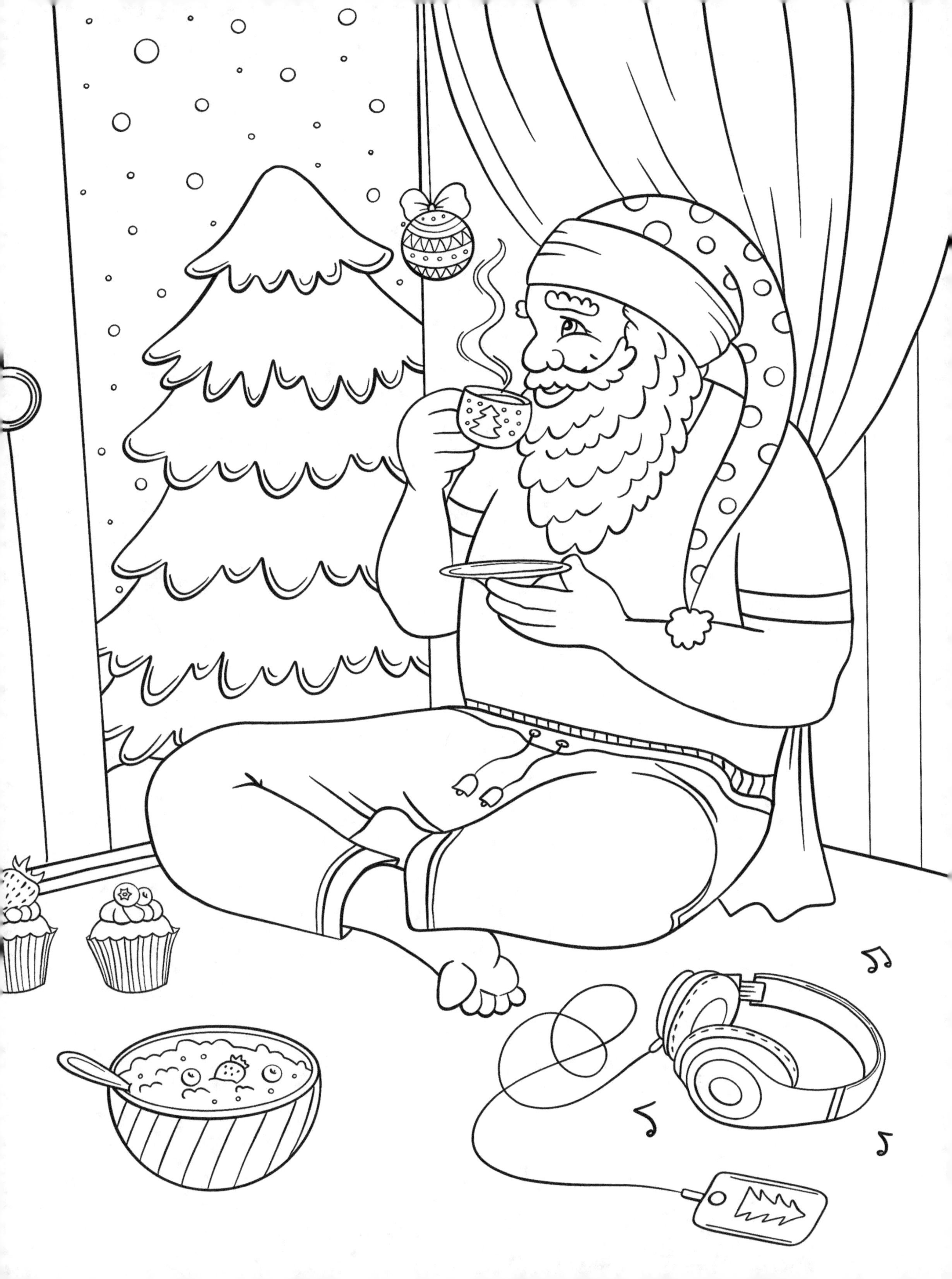

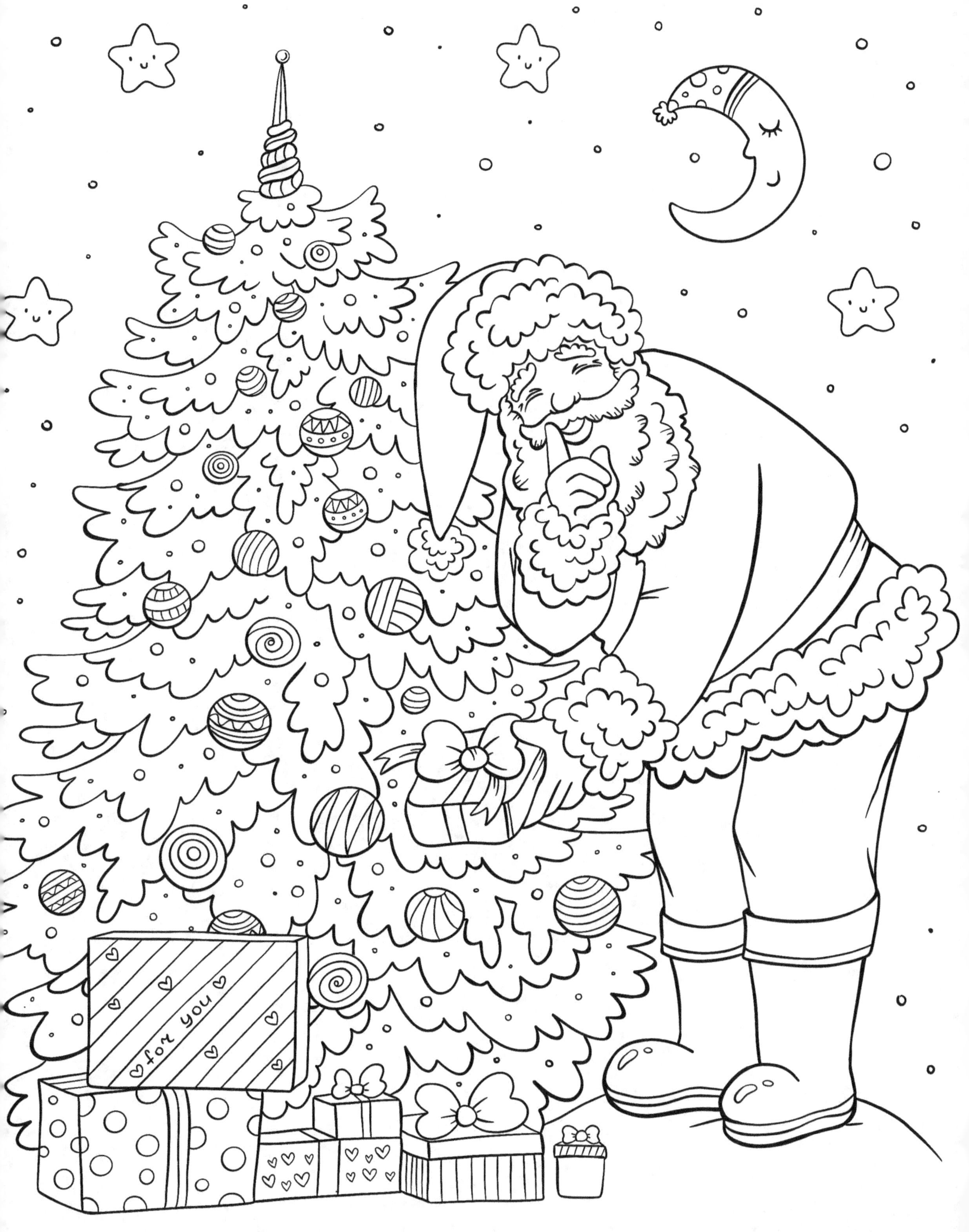
for you

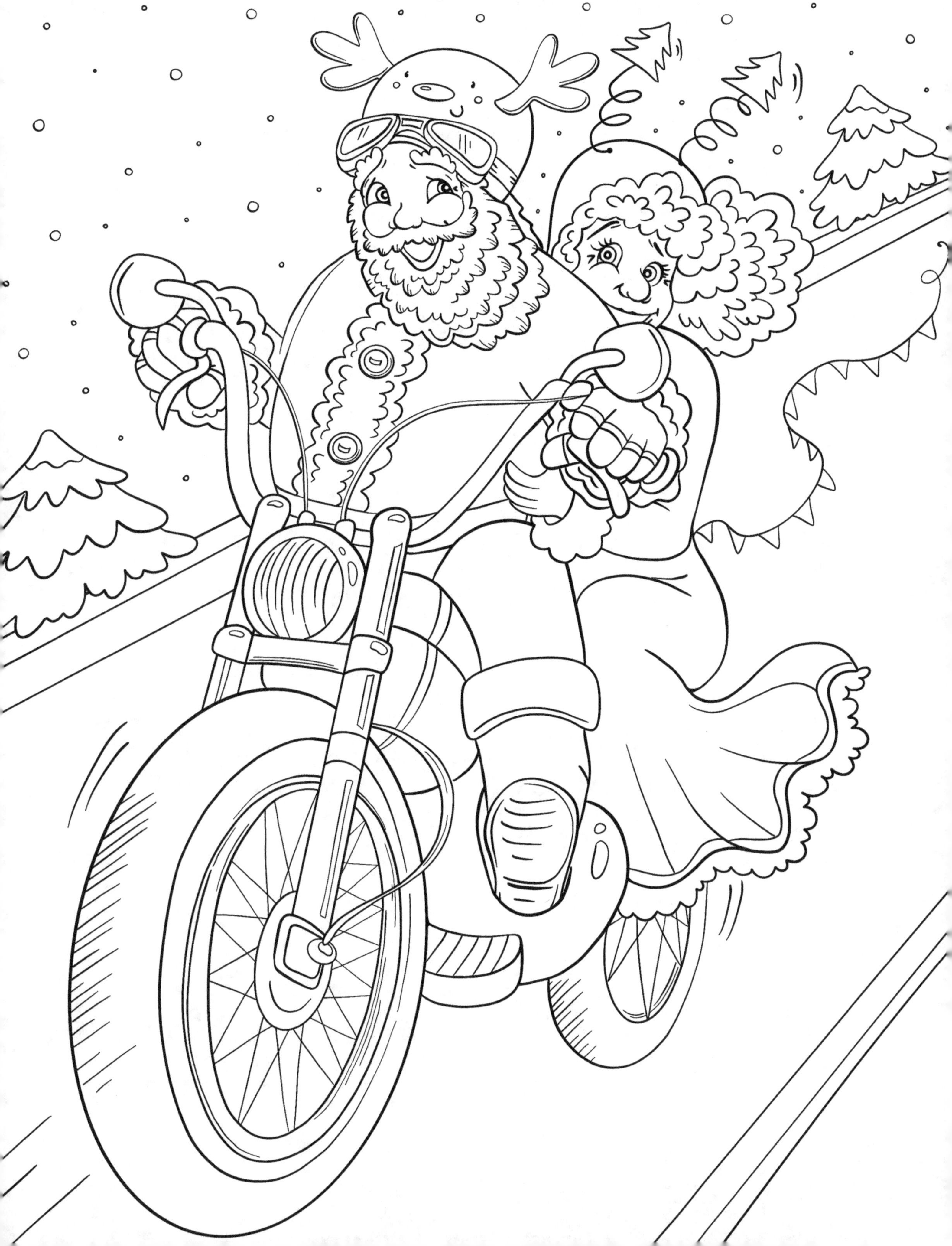

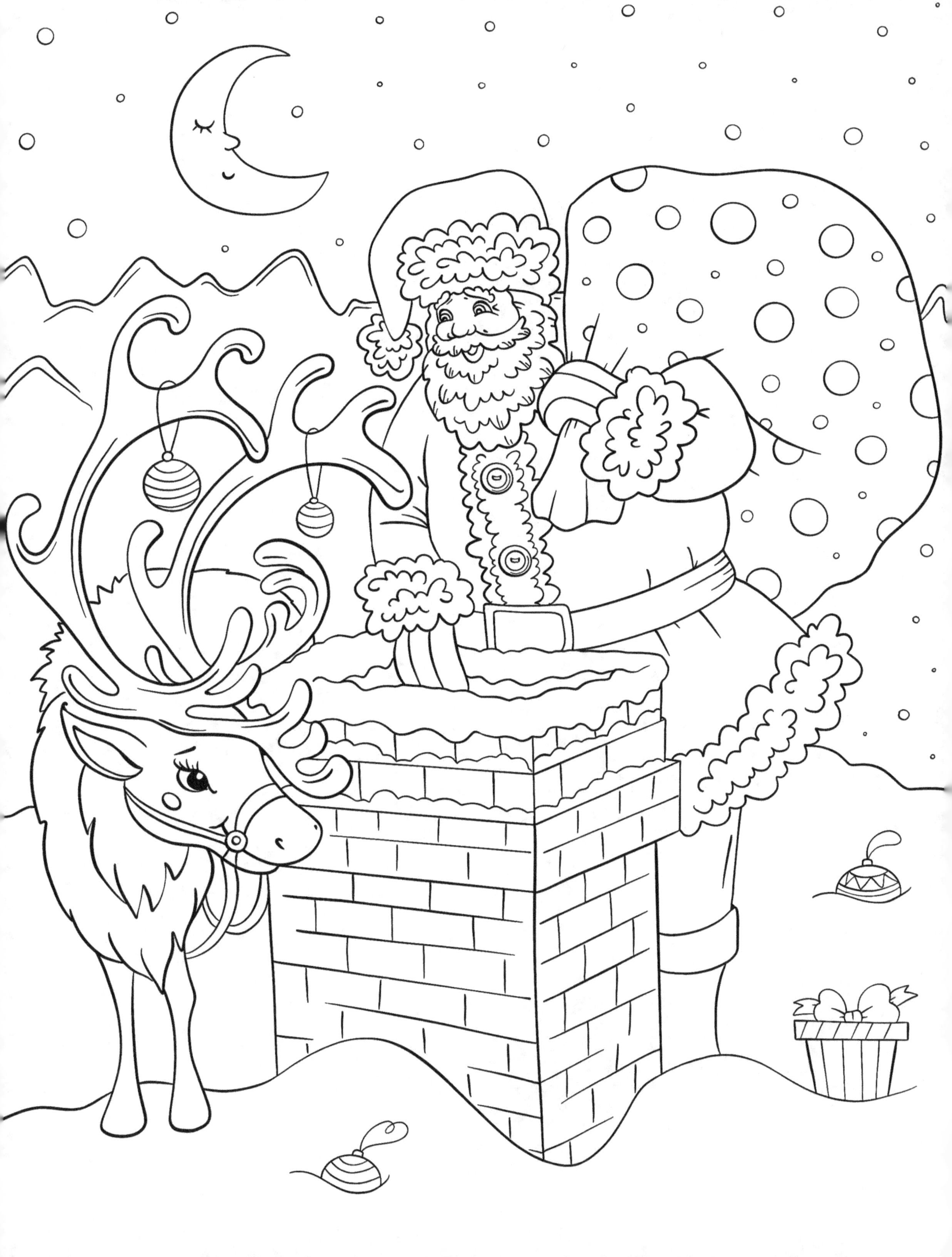

“We wish you a Merry Christmas and Happy New Year!”

List of gifts for loved ones for Christmas and New Year:

www.ingramcontent.com/pod-product-compliance
Lightning Source LLC
Chambersburg PA
CBHW081709220526
45466CB00009B/2923
* 9 7 8 1 6 7 4 8 0 1 4 8 3 *